BIGGEST NAMES IN SPORTS

MAYA MOORE

BASKETBALL STAR

WITHDRAWN

by Matt Scheff

FOCUS
READERS

WWW.FOCUSREADERS.COM

Focus Readers is distributed by North Star Editions:
sales@northstareditions.com | 888-417-0195

Produced for Focus Readers by Red Line Editorial.

Photographs ©: Pablo Martinez Monsivais/AP Images, cover, 1; AJ Mast/AP Images, 4–5, 7; Charlotte B. Teagle/Atlanta Journal-Constitution/AP Images, 8–9; Jessica Hill/AP Images, 11, 23; Mark Duncan/AP Images, 13; Tom Olmscheid/AP Images, 14–15; Stacy Bengs/AP Images, 17, 20–21, 27; John Bazemore/AP Images, 19; Charlie Neibergall/AP Images, 25; Red Line Editorial, 29

Library of Congress Cataloging-in-Publication Data
Library of Congress Cataloging-in-Publication Data is available on the Library of Congress website.

ISBN
978-1-64185-321-7 (hardcover)
978-1-64185-379-8 (paperback)
978-1-64185-495-5 (ebook pdf)
978-1-64185-437-5 (hosted ebook)

Printed in the United States of America
Mankato, MN
October, 2018

ABOUT THE AUTHOR

Matt Scheff is an artist and author living in Alaska. He enjoys mountain climbing, deep-sea fishing, and curling up with his two Siberian huskies to watch basketball.

TABLE OF CONTENTS

CHAPTER 1

BUZZER-BEATER

Everyone in the building knew who would be getting the ball. More than 16,000 Indiana Fever fans watched nervously. The Minnesota Lynx prepared to throw the ball in bounds. It was Game 3 of the 2015 WNBA Finals. Only 1.7 seconds remained on the clock. The game was tied 77–77.

Moore launches a three-pointer in the closing seconds of Game 3 of the 2015 WNBA Finals.

The Lynx needed someone to make a big play. And there was no one better suited for the job than Minnesota's star player, Maya Moore. She was at her best under pressure.

Moore ran toward the three-point line. From there, she took the pass. Moore faked a shot. That drew her defender into the air. Now Moore was wide open. She calmly took one dribble to her right. Then she launched a high-arcing shot.

The ball dropped through the net just as the final buzzer sounded. Minnesota had won! The stunned Indiana fans looked on as Moore's teammates mobbed her near center court.

Moore and her Lynx teammates celebrate after winning Game 3 of the 2015 WNBA Finals.

Moore's **buzzer-beater** helped the Lynx take a 2–1 lead in the series. They went on to win the series 3–2. It was their third championship in five years. Moore had been with the team for all three of them. She was the **centerpiece** of the league's best team.

CHAPTER 2

COLLEGE STAR

Maya Moore was born on June 11, 1989, in Jefferson City, Missouri. She was a very active child. When Maya was just three years old, her mother put a basketball hoop on the door of their apartment. It was the start of a lifelong love of basketball.

Maya Moore attempts a layup during a 2003 high school game with Collins Hill.

Over the years, Maya grew into an excellent athlete. She played basketball and ran track. As a freshman at Collins Hill High School, she was already a starter on the basketball team. Maya watched the Women's National Basketball Association (WNBA). She dreamed of playing in the league someday.

By the time Maya was a junior, she was one of the best high school players in the United States. In 2006, she won the Naismith Prep Player of the Year Award. Then she won it again in 2007. She was only the second player to win the award twice. Maya led Collins Hill to three state championships in a row.

Maya Moore dribbles past a defender during a 2007 game with the Connecticut Huskies.

After high school, Moore went to the University of Connecticut. She had a basketball **scholarship**. The Connecticut Huskies were already one of the best women's basketball teams in the nation.

Moore made them even better. As a freshman, she averaged 17.8 points per game. She was also named the Big East Conference 2008 Player of the Year.

Moore and the Huskies went on to **dominate** women's college basketball. They went undefeated in both 2009 and 2010. They won the NCAA title both years. In her four-year college career, Moore's Huskies had an incredible record of 150–4. During one stretch between 2008 and 2010, they won 90 games in a row.

It seemed that there was nothing Moore couldn't do on the court. She was a great shooter and could slash

Moore tries to grab a loose ball during the 2011 NCAA tournament.

to the basket. She was a good passer, rebounder, and defender. Her fans couldn't wait to see how her skills would serve her in the WNBA.

Moore attended the 2011 WNBA **Draft**. The Minnesota Lynx had the first pick. No one was surprised when they used it to select Moore. Her dream was coming true. She was heading to the WNBA.

CHAPTER 3

WNBA CHAMPIONSHIPS

The top pick in the draft usually goes to a team that is struggling. But that wasn't the case for Maya Moore and the Lynx. Minnesota had a young and talented roster. Fans hoped Moore would be the piece that would push the team deep into the WNBA playoffs.

Moore leaps past a Los Angeles Sparks defender during her rookie season.

Moore didn't disappoint them. In 2011, the 6-foot (183 cm) forward averaged 13.2 points per game. Those numbers helped her win WNBA **Rookie** of the Year honors. The Lynx finished with the best record in the league and advanced to

PLAYING OVERSEAS

Moore also plays outside of the United States. WNBA stars don't make the huge salaries that NBA players do. For this reason, many of them go overseas to play during the offseason. From 2012 to 2015, Moore played for the Shanxi Flame in China. She led the team to three straight Women's Chinese Basketball Association titles. Moore was hugely popular in China. Fans called her the Invincible Queen.

Moore attempts to steal the ball during the 2011 WNBA Finals.

the WNBA Finals. There, they faced the Atlanta Dream.

Moore and the Lynx were unstoppable in the Finals. They beat Atlanta three games to none to claim Minnesota's first WNBA title. Moore knocked down a big three-point basket in the final game. That shot helped seal the victory for the Lynx.

The Lynx returned to the WNBA Finals in 2012. However, they lost to the Indiana Fever. That same year, Moore was a member of the US Women's Olympic team. Moore and her teammates earned gold by beating France 86–50 in the final game.

Moore and the Lynx were back in the WNBA Finals in 2013. It was their third straight trip. They faced the Dream once again. And this time, Moore was at her best. She scored 23 points in Game 3 and led Minnesota to its second title. The Lynx were practically unstoppable that year. They didn't lose a single game in the playoffs.

Moore and the Lynx celebrate their second title in three years after winning the 2013 WNBA Finals.

Off the court, Moore displayed a friendly, easygoing personality. That made her one of the WNBA's most popular players. Several companies even hired her to **endorse** their products. More and more people were becoming fans of basketball superstar Maya Moore.

CHAPTER 4

BUILDING A DYNASTY

The 2014 WNBA season may have been Maya Moore's best. She averaged 23.9 points and 8.1 rebounds per game. Both were career highs. She also scored 48 points in a single game, which was one of the highest totals in WNBA history. Best of all, she took home the Most Valuable Player (MVP) award.

Moore shoots a jumper in a 2014 playoff game against the Phoenix Mercury.

Moore accepted the award in her home arena before a crowd of roaring fans.

The season ended in disappointment, though. Moore and the Lynx lost to the Phoenix Mercury in the Western Conference Finals. For the first time in her pro career, Moore was not headed to the WNBA Finals.

The Lynx bounced back in 2015. Moore lit up the WNBA All-Star Game with 30 points. She was named the MVP of the game. Then the Lynx claimed their third championship with their thrilling five-game victory over the Fever. Moore's buzzer-beating shot in Game 3 was a big part of the reason why.

Moore attempts a layup during the 2015 WNBA All-Star Game.

Minnesota appeared to be cruising to another title in 2016. The Lynx rolled through the regular season. But they lost in the fifth game of the WNBA Finals on a buzzer-beater by the Los Angeles Sparks.

SOCIALLY MINDED

Moore uses her star status to make a difference in the world. She is involved in several faith-based charities. She also works with programs that promote literacy. In addition, Moore speaks out on social issues. For instance, she has been critical of the criminal justice system in the United States. In 2016, she protested a police shooting by wearing a black t-shirt. The shirt read, "Change Starts With Us: Justice & Accountability."

Moore pulls down a rebound in a game against France during the 2016 Summer Olympics.

It was a tough loss for Moore. But she was determined to win another title.

Moore returned to the Olympics in 2016. And once again, she and her teammates took home gold. It was a proud moment for Team USA.

In 2017, Moore and the Lynx sealed their place as the greatest **dynasty** in WNBA history. They finished with the league's best record. They also made it back to the Finals. For the second year in a row, their opponent was Los Angeles.

The Sparks jumped out to a 2–1 series lead. But Moore and her teammates battled back to win Game 4. Now it all came down to Game 5. Moore scored a team-best 18 points as Minnesota notched an 85–76 victory. The Lynx were champions again! Moore and her teammates celebrated their fourth WNBA title. With that total, they were tied for most in league history.

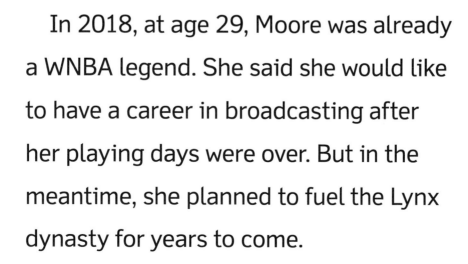

Moore drives toward the basket during Game 1 of the 2017 WNBA Finals.

In 2018, at age 29, Moore was already a WNBA legend. She said she would like to have a career in broadcasting after her playing days were over. But in the meantime, she planned to fuel the Lynx dynasty for years to come.

MAYA MOORE

- Height: 6 feet 0 inches (183 cm)
- Weight: 178 pounds (81 kg)
- Birth date: June 11, 1989
- Birthplace: Jefferson City, Missouri
- High school: Collins Hill (Suwanee, Georgia)
- College: University of Connecticut (Storrs, Connecticut) (2007–2011)
- WNBA team: Minnesota Lynx (Minneapolis, Minnesota) (2011–)
- Major awards: WNBA champion (2011, 2013, 2015, 2017); WNBA MVP (2014); WNBA Finals MVP (2013); NCAA champion (2009–2010); Naismith College Player of the Year (2009, 2011)

Minneapolis

Storrs

Jefferson City

Suwanee

FOCUS ON
MAYA MOORE

Write your answers on a separate piece of paper.

1. Write a paragraph summarizing the main ideas of Chapter 3.

2. Do you think Moore would say 2014 was her best season? Why or why not?

3. Which team did the Lynx defeat in the 2013 WNBA Finals?

> **A.** Indiana Fever
> **B.** Los Angeles Sparks
> **C.** Atlanta Dream

4. Which game did Moore get a gold medal for winning?

> **A.** 2010 NCAA Championship
> **B.** 2016 Olympics
> **C.** 2017 WNBA Finals

Answer key on page 32.

GLOSSARY

buzzer-beater
A shot that goes through the rim with no time remaining on the clock.

centerpiece
The most important part of something.

dominate
To show that one player or team is clearly better than an opponent.

draft
A system that allows teams to acquire new players coming into a league.

dynasty
A team that has a long run of winning championships.

endorse
To publicly support or speak in favor of a product.

literacy
The ability to read and write.

rookie
A professional athlete in his or her first year.

scholarship
Money given to a student to pay for education expenses.

TO LEARN MORE

BOOKS

Ervin, Phil. *12 Reasons to Love Basketball*. Mankato, MN: 12-Story Library, 2018.

Ervin, Phil. *Maya Moore*. Minneapolis: Abdo Publishing, 2016.

Mortensen, Lori. *Maya Moore: Basketball Star*. North Mankato, MN: Capstone Press, 2018.

NOTE TO EDUCATORS

Visit **www.focusreaders.com** to find lesson plans, activities, links, and other resources related to this title.

INDEX

Answer Key: 1. Answers will vary; **2.** Answers will vary; **3.** C; **4.** B